GRADE

3

Fluency FIRST!™

Timothy Rasinski • Nancy Padak

Mc Graw Hill **Wright Group**

The **McGraw·Hill** Companies

www.WrightGroup.com

 **Wright Group**

Fluency First! Daily Routines to Develop Reading Fluency: Grade 3
Copyright ©2005 Wright Group/McGraw-Hill

Created by Kent Publishing Services, Inc.
Designed by Signature Design Group, Inc.
Illustrations by Shirely Beckes, Nelle Davis, Steve Sullivan

The publishers would like to acknowledge the authors and publishers of the following copyrighted works, which appear in *Fluency First!* Grade 3 Student Book. Page 16, "Super Sampson Simpson" by Jack Prelutsky, Text copyright © 1990 by Jack Prelutsky. Used by permission of HarperCollins Publishers; page 18, "Last Night I Dreamed of Chickens" by Jack Prelutsky, Text copyright © 1990 by Jack Prelutsky. Used by permission of HarperCollins Publishers; page 30, "Let's Make a Salad" by Sonja Dunn, Pembroke Publishers; page 38, "Going to School" by Maria Morales, Visual Education Corporation; page 40, "My First Days in New York" by Herman Badillo, Visual Education Corporation; page 42, "My First Days in First Grade" by Francisco Jimenez; page 44, "I've Got a Cold" by Sonja Dunn, Pembroke Publishers; page 46, "The Blanket Doesn't Feel Right" by Sonja Dunn, Pembroke Publishers; page 66, "Why Possum's Tail is Bare" by George F. Scheer III; page 80, "Rainy Day" translated by Ayako Egawa, from the Japanese song "Amefuri." Words by Mr. Hakushu Kitahra and music by Mr. Shinpei Nakayama. Translated into "Rainy Day" by Ms. Ayako Egawa; page 88, excerpt from Sounder by William H. Armstrong. Text copyright ©1969 by William H. Armstrong. Used by permission of HarperCollins Publishers; page 90, "How to Tell the Wild Animals" by Carolyn Wells; page 98, "The Dream Keeper" by Langston Hughes; page 112, "The Mess" by Brod Bagert; page 114, "Puppy Disobedience" by Brod Bagert; page 128, from *Space Songs* by Myra Cohn Livingston, "Jewels" from *Space Songs* by Myra Cohn Livingston. Copyright © 1988 by Myra Cohn Livingston. Used by permission of Marian Reiner.; page 130, quotation from *I Know Why the Caged Bird Sings* by Maya Angelou. Used with permission from Random House, and quotations included in "Who is Maya Angelou?" by Maya Angelou.

Printed in the United States of America.

Send all inquiries to:
Wright Group/McGraw-Hill
P.O. Box 812960
Chicago, IL 60681

ISBN: 1-4045-2666-8

10 9 8 7 6 5

Table of Contents

Table of Contents *continued*

Introduction

This is How Fluency First! Lessons Work

 **Listen**

---

2 **Read Along**

---

3 **Practice in Class**

 Practice at Home

 Build Your Skills

 Perform

Parade

Sometimes I'm scared to stand and speak.
My voice turns into a little squeak.

I'll try to talk then get afraid,
But if I pretend I'm in a parade,

Then my voice is loud and clear
saying "right" and "left" for all to hear.

I lead the march along the way,
And never worry about what I'll say.

Left—right, left—right, left—right, march!

Sarah Hutt

How did I read?	How can I do better?
☺ ☺ ☹	

Odd Word Out

1. Circle the word in each group that does not rhyme.

speak	peek	clerk	cheek

were	deer	here	clear

afraid	playground	homemade	parade

Answer the Riddle

2. Write a word from the poem to answer each riddle.

I start with a blend and rhyme with **hand**. _____

I start with a blend and sound like a mouse. _____

My vowel sound is the same as in **joy** and **boy**. _____

I rhyme with **crowd** and tell how a crowd can sound. _____

Name the Feeling

3. Write words from the box below that name the feelings expressed in the poem.

fear	worry	anger	love
sadness	hope	happiness	dislike

_____

_____

Summer Grass

Summer grass aches and whispers.

It wants something; it calls and sings; it pours
    out wishes to the overhead stars.
The rain hears; the rain answers; the rain is slow
    coming; the rain wets the face of the grass.

Carl Sandburg

How did I read?	How can I do better?

Make Compound Words

1. Add a word to each word below to make a compound word.
   Some of these compound words are from the poem.

   an unknown object   some_____

   an unknown person   some_____

   above you   over_____

   from evening until morning   over_____

   colors in the sky after a storm   rain_____

   something you wear in the rain   rain_____

Change the Word

2. Change or add one letter in the word **hear** to create
   new words.

   something that makes you warm   _____

   a large, furry animal that lives in the forest   _____

   not far   _____

   what you do with clothes   _____

   when a sore gets better, it does this   _____

   the body part that pumps your blood   _____

Guess Who?

I looked in the mirror
and what did I see
on the face that was there
looking back at me?

I saw cracker crumbs
and some strawberry jelly
on the chin and the cheek
and the shirt-covered belly.

And a large spot of soot
right there on the nose,
and a few more spots
here and there on the clothes.

What is your name?
Who can you be
inside of the mirror
looking out at me?

I filled up the sink
took the soap and began
washing my face and my
arms and my hands.

I put on a clean shirt
and combed my hair
and went to the mirror
to see who was there.

Who's in the mirror?
Who is that I see?
It's my own face
looking back at me!

Karen McGuigan Brothers.

How did I read?	How can I do better?

Odd Word Out

1. Circle the word in each group that does not rhyme.

nose	goose	chose	froze
see	like	me	flea
hair	wear	chair	car

Finish the Rhyme

2. Write a word to finish each rhyme.

I went in the bathroom
and took my place.
I brushed my teeth
and washed my _____.

I went in the kitchen
and who was there?
Someone new had
sat in my _____.

I went outside
to take a walk.
I met a friend
who said, "Let's _____."

Explain the Poem

3. Write one or two sentences that explain what happens in the poem.

_____

_____

_____

How Special I Am!

If I were a crow, I'd wear a big bow
so people would know how special I am.

If I were a deer, I'd stand up and cheer
so people would hear how special I am.

If I were a goat, I'd wear a red coat
so people would know how special I am.

If I were a bear, I'd send up a flare
to brightly declare how special I am.

But I'm not a crow who wears a big bow;
and I'm not a deer who shouts out a cheer;
and I'm not a goat who wears a red coat;
and I'm not a bear, and I don't have a flare.

I am just me; there's only one me
and it's plain to see how special I am.

Karen McGuigan Brothers

How did I read?	How can I do better?

Sounds the Same

1. Read the pairs of homophones and the sentences below.
   One word is from the poem. Write the correct homophone
   on the line to complete the sentence.

   know/no

   When my mom asked if I had any homework, I said _____.

   Do you _____ where my cookie is?

   deer/dear

   The _____ are eating the leaves off the trees.

   The letter began, "_____ Bobby."

   bear/bare

   Did you see a _____ in the woods?

   My _____ arms are cold!

Rhyming Words

2. Complete the chart by writing the rhyming words.

Words that rhyme with <u>crow</u>	Words that rhyme with <u>cow</u>
_____	_____
_____	_____

Super Samson Simpson

I am Super Samson Simpson,
I'm superlatively strong,
I like to carry elephants,
I do it all day long,
I pick up half a dozen
and hoist them in the air,
it's really somewhat simple,
for I have strength to spare.

My muscles are enormous,
they bulge from top to toe,
and when I carry elephants,
they ripple to and fro,
but I am not the strongest
in the Simpson family,
for when I carry elephants,
my grandma carries me.

Jack Prelutsky

How did I read?	How can I do better?

Match the Definitions

1. Draw a line to match each word from the poem with its definition.

hoist   to stick out

enormous   to rise and fall

superlatively   the most

dozen   to lift

bulge   twelve

ripple   huge

Draw It

2. Draw a picture of Super Samson Simpson lifting an elephant based on the poem. Write a sentence underneath to explain it.

Last Night I Dreamed of Chickens

Last night I dreamed of chickens,
there were chickens everywhere,
they were standing on my stomach,
they were nesting in my hair,
they were pecking at my pillow,
they were hopping on my head,
they were ruffling up their feathers
as they raced about my bed.

They were on the chairs and tables,
they were on the chandeliers,
they were roosting in the corners,
they were clucking in my ears,
there were chickens, chickens, chickens
for as far as I could see...
when I woke today, I noticed
there were eggs on top of me.

Jack Prelutsky

How did I read?	How can I do better?
☺ ☺ ☹	

Base Words

1. Sometimes the spelling of a word changes when an ending is added.
   Each word below is from the poem. Write the word without its ending.

   dreamed   _____

   standing   _____

   hopping   _____

   ruffling   _____

   raced   _____

   roosting   _____

   clucking   _____

   noticed   _____

Middle Sounds

2. When the letters **c** and **k** appear together in the middle of a
   word they make the sound of **k**. List the words from the poem
   that have **ck** in the middle.

   _____

   _____

   _____

The Table and the Chair

Said the Table to the Chair,
"You can hardly be aware
How I suffer from the heat
And from blisters on my feet.
If we took a little walk;
We might have a little talk;
Yes, let us take the air,"
Said the Table to the Chair.

Said the Chair unto the Table,
"Now, you *know* we are not able:
How foolishly you talk,
When you know we *cannot* walk!"
Said the Table with a sigh,
"It can do no harm to try.
I've as many legs as you:
Why can't we walk on two?"

Edward Lear

How did I read?	How can I do better?
☺ ☺ ☹	

Word Meanings

1. Write each word from the poem after its meaning.

suffer	harm	hardly	blisters	sigh

breathe out a long breath _____

wounded skin _____

scarcely _____

feel distress _____

damage _____

Compare the Furniture

2. Use the Venn diagram to compare the Table and Chair
from the poem.

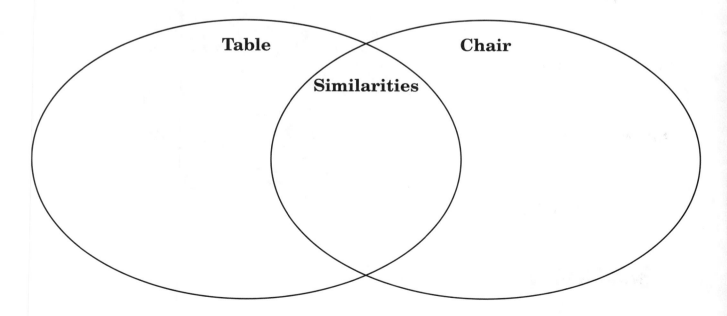

A Limerick

There was an Old Man with a beard,
Who said, "It is just as I feared!—
Two Owls and a Hen,
Four Larks and a Wren,
Have all built their nests in my beard!"

Edward Lear

How did I read?	How can I do better?

Synonyms and Antonyms

1. The first word in each pair is from the limerick. Read each word pair. Then write whether the words are synonyms (alike) or antonyms (opposites).

just	exactly	_____
man	woman	_____
all	none	_____
hen	chicken	_____
old	young	_____

Write About

2. Look at the picture of the Old Man. Write a description of him.

_____

_____

_____

_____

_____

_____

_____

from John Henry

When John Henry was about three days old,
Just a-sittin' on his pappy's knee,
He gave one loud and lonesome cry:
"The hammer'll be the death of me,
The hammer'll be the death of me."

Well, the captain said to John Henry one day:
"Gonna bring that steam drill out on the job,
Gonna whop that steel on down,
Gonna whop that steel on down."

John Henry said to the captain:
"Well, a man ain't nothin' but a man,
and before I let a steam drill beat me down,
Gonna die with the hammer in my hand."

John Henry went to the tunnel,
and they put him in the lead to drive;
the rock so tall and John Henry so small,
He laid down his hammer and he cried.

American work song

How did I read?	How can I do better?
☺ ☺ ☹	

What Is the Story?

1. The song tells a story. Who is the song about?

_____

2. What problem does the main character face?

_____

3. What does the character do?

_____

Apostrophes

4. Write the word or words that match these words from "John Henry."

nothin'   _____

sittin'   _____

hammer'll   _____

Opposites

5. Write a word that is the opposite of each of these words from "John Henry."

tall   _____

loud   _____

down   _____

small   _____

from John Henry

Well, the man that invented the steam drill,
He thought he was mighty fine,
But John Henry drove his fifteen feet,
And the steam drill only made nine.

John Henry looked up at the mountain,
And his hammer was striking fire,
Well, he hammered so hard
    that he broke his poor old heart,
He laid down his hammer and he died.

They took John Henry to the graveyard,
And they laid him in the sand;
Three men from the east
    and a woman from the west
Came to see that old steel-drivin' man.

They took John Henry to the graveyard,
And they laid him in the sand,
And every locomotive come a-roarin' by
Says: "There lies a steel drivin' man."

American work song

How did I read?	How can I do better?

Write Synonyms

1. Write a synonym from the box for each of these words from "John Henry."

great   placed   ancient   created

fine _____

invented _____

laid _____

old _____

How Many Syllables?

2. Write the number of syllables that are in each of these words from "John Henry."

woman _____   hammer _____

sand _____   locomotive _____

mountain _____   fifteen _____

Write a Description

3. Write a sentence that tells what John Henry was like. Use adjectives in your sentence.

_____

from The Camel's Complaint

Lambs are enclosed where it's never exposed,
Coops are constructed for hens;
Kittens are treated to houses well heated,
And pigs are protected by pens.
But a camel comes handy
Wherever it's sandy—
Anywhere does for me.

Cats, you're aware, can repose in a chair,
Chickens can roost upon rails;
Puppies are able to sleep in a stable,
And oysters can slumber in pails.
But no one supposes
A poor camel dozes—
Anyplace does for me.

People would laugh if you rode a giraffe,
Or mounted the back of an ox;
It's nobody's habit to ride on a rabbit,
Or try to bestraddle a fox.
But as for a camel, he's
Ridden by families—
Any load does for me.

Charles E. Carryl

How did I read?	How can I do better?

Finding Rhymes

1. Write down the rhyming words for each stanza.

Stanza 1

enclosed   _____

treated   _____

Stanza 2

aware   _____

able   _____

Stanza 3

laugh   _____

habit   _____

Animals Everywhere

2. Write the name of six animals that appear in the poem. Next to the animal name, write some words that describe the animal.

Animal name	Words that describe the animal
_____	_____
_____	_____
_____	_____
_____	_____
_____	_____
_____	_____

Let's Make a Salad

First you wash the lettuce
Then you spin it dry
Chop a lot of onions
till they make you cry
If you want a salad
that's the best you've had
all you have to do is
     ADD
pepper and lime
parsley and thyme
a dash of salt too
makes dressing for you
     THEN
Slice in a tomato
Add a bit of cheese
Salad in a bowl
Serve it
if you please!

Sonja Dunn

How did I read?	How can I do better?

Rhyming Words

1. For each word, write down the words in the poem that rhyme with it. Then add a rhyming word of your own.

dry _____ _____

had _____ _____

lime _____ _____

too _____ _____

cheese _____ _____

Food Fun

2. Write the name of each ingredient that goes into the salad. Circle each food you like. Place an **X** over each food you don't like.

_____ _____ _____

_____ _____ _____

_____ _____ _____

Does Not Belong

3. List ten foods you would probably *never* find in a real salad.

_____ _____ _____

_____ _____ _____

_____ _____ _____

Late

Today I missed the bus.
This is how it happened.

I woke up on time.
I got dressed.
I went into the kitchen
    for breakfast.

First there was no cereal.
Then the muffins were moldy.
And when I tried to pour
    some orange juice,
    the carton was empty.

I gave up on breakfast
    and tried to find my shoes.
They weren't in my room
    or closet.
They weren't in the hallway.

So I gave up on shoes
    and found a pair of boots.
I grabbed my bag.
I ran to the bus stop.

Everyone was there,
    waiting for the bus.
I looked down at my bag.
It looked a little odd.

That's when it hit me:
I had grabbed my brother's
    bag instead of mine!
As I was running home to
    get the right one,
    the bus drove by.

And that is why I'm late.

Laura Portalupi

How did I read?	How can I do better?
☺ ☺ ☺	

Y Not?

1. The second stanza of the poem has two words that end in **-y**.
Describing words, or adjectives, often end in **-y**. Complete
each sentence with a word from the box.

scary	heavy	itchy	scratchy	lucky
silly	woolly	pretty	happy	

The box of books was very _____.

The TV show about the talking horse was _____.

The girl who won the spelling contest was _____.

The movie with the space aliens was _____.

The mother sheep was very _____.

Mom's new dress is really _____.

I was _____ to win the door prize.

When Dad forgets to shave, his beard is _____.

My mosquito bites are really _____.

Replacing Words

2. Read the sentence from the poem. Replace the underlined words
with words of your own that make sense in your new sentence.

I went into the <u>kitchen</u> for <u>breakfast</u>.

I went into the _____ for _____.

My Cat Ate My Homework

My cat ate my homework.
She really did.

Let me explain.

For my class experiment,
I was growing a plant.

Last month I planted a seed.
It grew into a little green sprout.
It grew tiny green leaves.

I guess my cat was very hungry last night.
She jumped onto the windowsill.
She started nibbling on my plant!

"Stop!" I yelled.
But it was too late.
She was happily chewing on my little plant!

And that is how the cat ate my homework.

Laura Portalupi

How did I read?	How can I do better?
☺ ☺ ☹	

Words that Tell How

1. Words that describe how something is done often end in **-ly**.
Use each of the **-ly** words below in a sentence of your own.

really _____

happily _____

badly _____

loudly _____

quietly _____

softly _____

Then What Happened?

2. Use the chart below to list what happened in the poem.

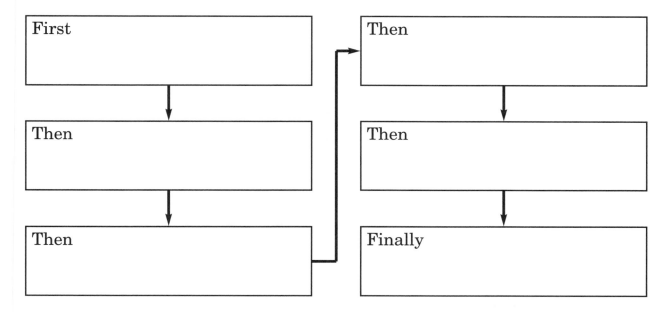

First

Then

Then

Then

Then

Finally

Our Flag

I love to see the starry flag
that floats above my head.
I love to see its waving folds
With stripes of white and red.

"Be brave," say the red stripes,
"Be pure," say the white.
"Be true," say the bright stars,
"And stand for the right."

Author unknown

How did I read?	How can I do better?
☺ ☺ ☹	

Finding Rhymes

1. The words at the ends of lines 2 and 4 rhyme. So do the
   words at the ends of lines 6 and 8. Fill in the blanks with
   more words that rhyme.

Rhymes with <u>head</u> and <u>red</u>	Rhymes with <u>white</u> and <u>right</u>
_____	_____
_____	_____
_____	_____
_____	_____
_____	_____

All the Best Words

2. List the words in the poem that begin with **st-**. Then add
   more words that also begin with this letter combination.

Words in the poem with <u>st-</u>	Other words with <u>st-</u>
_____	_____
_____	_____
_____	_____
_____	_____

Going to School

Maria Morales tells what it was like when she came with her family to the United States many years ago.

We came in June 1923.... And we tried to learn English as fast as we could, which we did.... It was no disgrace to be poor.... We were Mexicans, there was no way to beat it. In fact, our skin is different, our cultures were different. [We had] to accept it and be proud. That's the way we were raised.

So when we went to school if anybody...[said], "You eat tortillas"...they were saying the truth. Because we did have tortillas and we did have beans...so we learned not to get mad at them. It hurt...but we just grew up that way.

...We tried to excel in our studies. That was our way of recompensating...we were proud to be Mexican.

Maria Morales

How did I read?	How can I do better?
☺ ☺ ☺	

Write About

1. Write a sentence using the words **tortillas** and **beans**.

_____

Syllable Break

2. Say each word. Write the number of syllables you hear.

English _____ disgrace _____

Mexican _____ culture _____

excel _____ accept _____

different _____ tortillas _____

anybody _____ studies _____

learned _____ recompensation _____

Homophones

3. Homophones sound the same but have different spellings. Write a word from the selection next to its homophone below.

bee _____ beet _____

know _____ witch _____

My First Days in New York

Herman Badillo came from Puerto Rico to New York City in 1941. He became a member of the U.S. Congress. This is what he remembered about his first days in New York City.

I thought I had come into Paradise. I had been starving for seven years, and now I got three meals and could eat my fill. I had a pair of shoes. What made the greatest impression on me was that people did not seem to be hungry, and instead of the widespread unemployment I saw all around me in Puerto Rico, most people seemed to have work. This alone was enough to impress me.

Herman Badillo

How did I read?	How can I do better?
☺ ☺ ☹	

Proper Nouns

1. Write the proper nouns on the lines below.
Include names of people and places.

_____   _____

_____   _____

_____

Antonyms

2. Write a word from the selection that means the opposite
of each word below.

nonmember _____

forgot _____

full _____

limited _____

unemployment _____

Point of View

3. What impressed the speaker of the selection the most
about New York City? Circle the correct answer.

People had jobs.   People had shoes.   People ate healthy food.

My First Days in First Grade

The Circuit, by Francisco Jimenez, is a collection of stories from the author's childhood. His parents were migrant farmers, so they frequently moved from one place to another. When he was young, Francisco went to school without knowing any English. This is his description of his first few days in first grade.

Miss Scalapino started speaking to the class and I did not understand a word she was saying. The more she spoke, the more anxious I became. By the end of the day, I was very tired of hearing Miss Scalapino talk because the sounds made no sense to me. I thought that perhaps by paying close attention, I would begin to understand, but I did not. I only got a headache, and that night, when I went to bed, I heard her voice in my head.

Francisco Jimenez

How did I read?	How can I do better?
☺	

Change the Ending

1. Make the following words plural by changing the
–**y** ending to –**ies**.

story   _____

family   _____

baby   _____

fairy   _____

Compound Words

2. Divide the following compound words. Write the word
parts on the lines below.

childhood   _____   _____

understand   _____   _____

headache   _____   _____

Add the Ending

3. Add –**tion** to the end of these words to make words from
the selection. You may have to change the spellings.

collect   _____

describe   _____

attend   _____

I've Got a Cold

I've got a cold
And I don't like it
No, I don't like it
Not one bit

When you catch a cold
and it's in your head
your nose gets plugged
your eyes turn red

You can't taste your food
'cause it hurts your throat
Your ears get plugged
and you can't sing a note

You cough and sneeze
and gasp and wheeze
You have a fever
That weakens your knees

There isn't much that you can do
but keep yourself warm
and drink a hot brew
And sleep a lot when you get into bed—

Just pull those covers
right over your head

Sonja Dunn

How did I read?	How can I do better?

Silent Letters

1. Find five words from the poem that have a **silent e** at the end. Write them on the lines.

_____   _____

_____   _____

_____

How to Treat a Cold

2. Draw three pictures showing what the poem suggests to do when you have a cold.

Keep yourself warm	Drink hot brew	Sleep a lot

The Blanket Doesn't Feel Right

I heard a noise in the basement
It gave me quite a fright!
And I don't want to go to bed now
'cause the blanket doesn't feel right

On a scary night, on a scary night
the blanket doesn't feel right!

I saw a creepy shadow
It was a spooky sight!
And I don't want to go to bed now
'cause the blanket doesn't feel right

On a scary night, on a scary night
The blanket doesn't feel right!

There's someone in the attic
It's dark and there's no light!
And I don't want to go to bed now
'cause the blanket doesn't feel right

On a scary night, on a scary night
the blanket doesn't feel right!

Sonja Dunn

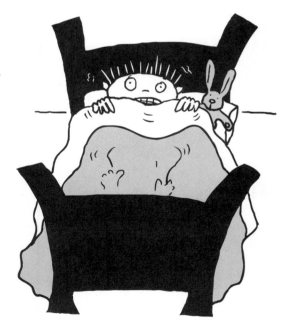

How did I read?	How can I do better?
☺ ☺/☹	

Word Families

1. Add letters to the beginning of **–ight** to make five different rhyming words from the selection.

   _____ight   _____ight

   _____ight   _____ight

   _____ight

Means the Same

2. Write a contraction that means the same as each pair of words below.

   does not   _____   is not   _____

   will not   _____   are not   _____

   do not   _____   was not   _____

What Does it Mean?

3. Describe what the author means when she says, "the blanket doesn't feel right."

   _____

   _____

   _____

from Block City

What are you able to build with your blocks?
Castles and palaces, temples, and docks.
Rain may keep raining, and others go roam,
But I can be happy and building at home.

Let the sofa be mountains, the carpet be sea,
There I'll establish a city for me:
A kirk and a mill and a palace beside,
And a harbor as well where my vessels may ride.

Now I have done with it, down let it go!
All in a moment the town is laid low.
Block upon block lying scattered and free,
What is there left of my town by the sea?

Robert Louis Stevenson

How did I read?	How can I do better?
☺ ☺ ☺	

Spelling Patterns

1. Find words from the poem that have the **long o** vowel sound.

Long o sound spelled **o** _____

Long o sound spelled **ow** _____

Long o spelled **o-consonant-e** _____

Building Names

2. Write words from the poem that name types of buildings.

_____   _____

_____   _____

_____   _____

Synonyms

3. Draw a line to match each word from the poem with its synonym.

couch	wander
build	make
roam	sofa
sea	boats
vessels	ocean

If My Shoes Could Talk

If my shoes could talk
I guess they would say
they've done a lot
of things today.

They walked along
the garden wall;
they jumped and ran
to catch a ball.

They hopped and shuffled
they danced and skipped,
they pedaled my bike,
they almost tripped.

They clung to my skateboard
through the sidewalks of town
and walked through a puddle
with mud all around.

If my shoes could talk,
I know they would say
they've had a very
busy day!

Karen McGuigan Brothers

How did I read?	How can I do better?
☺ ☺ ☺	

Syllable Count

1. Write words from the poem that have two syllables.

_____   _____

_____   _____

_____   _____

_____   _____

_____   _____

_____   _____

Find the Verbs

2. Write words from the poem that are verbs (action words).

_____   _____

_____   _____

_____   _____

_____   _____

_____   _____

Boys and Girls Come Out to Play

Boys and girls come out to play,
The moon doth shine as bright as day.
Leave your supper and leave your sleep,
And join your playfellows in the street.

Come with a whoop and come with a call,
Come with a good will or not at all.
Up the ladder and down the wall,
A half-penny loaf will serve us all;

You find milk, and I'll find flour,
And we'll have pudding in half an hour.

Nursery rhyme

How did I read?	How can I do better?
☺	

Spelling Patterns

1. Write words from the poem that have the **long e** vowel sound.

Long e vowel sound spelled **ee** _____

_____

Long e vowel sound spelled **ea** _____

Long e vowel sound spelled **y** _____

Homophones

2. Write homophones from the poem—words that sound like those below but are spelled differently. Then use both homophones to write a sentence.

- too _____

_____

- flower _____

_____

- our _____

_____

The Kind Moon

I think the moon is very kind
To take such trouble just for me.
He came along with me from home
To keep me company.

He went as fast as I could run;
I wonder how he crossed the sky?
I'm sure he hasn't legs and feet
Or any wings to fly.

Yet here he is above their roof;
Perhaps he thinks it isn't right
For me to go so far alone,
Tho' mother said I might.

Sara Teasdale

How did I read?	How can I do better?

Vowel Patterns

1. Write a word from the poem with the same vowel pattern as each word below. Then write another word with the same vowel pattern.

bright _____   _____

blind _____   _____

Contractions

2. Write contractions from the poem to match the words.
Write a sentence using each contraction.

- Is not _____

_____

- I am _____

_____

- has not _____

_____

Write About It

3. Write a sentence or two telling why the moon is "very kind."

_____

The Ant and the Grasshopper

One fine summer's day, Grasshopper sang and chirped as if he did not have a care in the world. Ant passed by, struggling to carry a large kernel of corn upon his back.

Grasshopper called to the busy Ant, "Come and sing with me for a while. It is too nice a day to be working!" Ant looked at Grasshopper.

"You do nothing but sing all day," he said.

"I do not have time to sing and play. I am storing up food for the long winter. I suggest you do, too."

Grasshopper laughed and said, "Why worry about winter? I have enough food for today."

Months passed. Winter had come and snow lay on the fields. Ant was happy. He had enough food to last until spring. But Grasshopper had nothing to eat.

"Ah," he said sadly, "I am so hungry. If only I had realized that it is best to prepare today for what I might need tomorrow."

Aesop, retold by Cynthia Hatch

How did I read?	How can I do better?

Past Tense

1. Write the past tense form of each verb to make a word from the poem. Then use the word to write a sentence.

- look   _____

_____

- chirp   _____

_____

- laugh   _____

_____

- pass   _____

_____

Write It

2. Write three words from the poem that are names for seasons.

_____

_____

_____

The Ant and the Dove

Narrator: It was a beautiful morning. An ant went to the river bank to get a drink of water. A little wave knocked him into the river.

Ant: Help! Help! The water is too fast. I'm going to drown!

Narrator: Even though he was yelling, the ant's voice was too soft to be heard. A dove was perched in a nearby tree. She saw the ant and knew he was in trouble.

Dove: I'll pull this leaf off the tree and drop it into the water. I hope the ant can cling to this and live!

Narrator: The ant climbed onto the leaf. He gave a great sigh. The leaf floated him safely to the water's edge.

Ant: Thank you, Dove. You saved my life.

Narrator: Days later, a bird catcher stopped by the dove's tree. He was very quiet. The man set a trap for the dove. The ant watched all of his actions very carefully.

Ant: I won't let him catch my friend. I'll bite him on the foot!

Narrator: The bird catcher cried out in pain. He dropped the trap. This sudden noise scared the dove away.

Dove: Thank you, ant. You saved my life.

Narrator: Always remember this lesson. *When you help a person—stranger or friend—the favor will be returned to you.*

Aesop, retold by Laura Portalupi

How did I read?	How can I do better?
☺ ☺ ☹	

Adding Endings

1. The word **carefully** in the fable is the base word **care** plus **–ful** and **–ly**. Add one or both of these endings to other words from the fable. What new words do you get? Write the new words in sentences to show the meanings.

- safe _____

_____

- quiet _____

_____

- pain _____   _____

_____

_____

Retell the Lesson

2. Write the fable's lesson in your own words.

_____

_____

_____

The Hare and the Tortoise

The Hare was once boasting of his speed in front of all the other animals. "I have never yet been beaten," said he, "when I put forth my full speed. I challenge any one here to race with me."

The Tortoise said quietly, "I accept your challenge."

"That is a good joke," said the Hare. "I could dance round you all the way."

"Keep your boasting till you've beaten me," answered the Tortoise. "Shall we race?"

So a course was fixed and a start was made. The Hare darted almost out of sight at once, but soon stopped and, to show his contempt for the Tortoise, lay down to have a nap. The Tortoise plodded on and plodded on, and when the Hare awoke from his nap, he saw the Tortoise just near the winning-post and could not run up in time to save the race. Then said the Tortoise:

"Plodding wins the race."

Aesop

How did I read?	How can I do better?
☺ ☺ ☹	

Character Sketch

1. What type of character is Hare? Write a few words to describe him. Draw a picture to go with your description.

_____

_____

_____

_____

2. Now write a few words and draw a picture for Tortoise. Use as many descriptive words as you can.

_____

_____

_____

_____

In Other Words

3. If a friend asked you to explain the lesson, "Plodding wins the race," what would you say? Write your response to your friend.

_____

_____

_____

The Milkmaid and Her Pail

Patty the Milkmaid was going to market carrying her milk in a pail on her head. As she went along she began thinking about what she would do with the money she would get for the milk.

"I'll buy some fowls from Farmer Brown," said she, "and they will lay eggs each morning, which I will sell to the parson's wife. With the money that I get from the sale of these eggs I'll buy myself a new dimity frock and a chip hat; and when I go to market, won't all the young men come up and speak to me! Polly Shaw will be that jealous; but I don't care. I shall just look at her and toss my head like this."

As she spoke she tossed her head back, the pail fell off it, and all the milk was spilt. So she had to go home and tell her mother what had occurred.

"Ah, my child," said the mother,

"Do not count your chickens before they are hatched."

Aesop

How did I read?	How can I do better?
☺ ☺ ☺	

Patty's Plans

1. What did Patty plan to do with the money she got for the milk?

_____

2. What did Patty plan to sell in order to buy new clothes?

_____

3. What ruined Patty's plans?

_____

Picture It

4. How does the fable end? What does Patty tell her mother?
What does her mother say? Draw a cartoon with Patty and
her mother and rewrite what they say in your own words.

from The Fisherman and His Wife

This is an excerpt from "The Fisherman and His Wife," a story by the Brothers Grimm. In this story, a fisherman and his wife are granted wishes by a prince disguised as a fish.

"Husband," said the wife, "have you caught anything today?"

"I caught a flounder," he replied, "who said he was an enchanted prince; so I threw him back into the water, and let him swim away."

"Did you not wish?" she asked.

"No," he said; "what should I wish for?"

"Why, at least for a better hut than this dirty place. How unlucky you did not think of it! Go and call him now; perhaps he will answer you."

When he saw how green and dark [the sea] looked, he felt much discouraged, but made up a rhyme and said:

"Flounder, flounder, in the sea,
Come, I beg, and talk to me;
For my wife, Dame Isabel,
Sent me here a tale to tell."

The Brothers Grimm

How did I read?	How can I do better?
☺ ☺ ☹	

Word Search

1. The word **unlucky** has the smaller words **luck** and **lucky** in it.
   Write the smaller words you find in these words from the story.

   anything   _____

   fisherman   _____

   discouraged   _____

   _____

About the Story

2. Why do you think the fisherman did not wish for anything?

   _____

   _____

3. Why did the fisherman become discouraged?

   _____

   _____

4. What did the fisherman do to make the fish return?

   _____

   _____

Why the Possum's Tail Is Bare

This is what the old men told me when I was young:

Possum used to have a long, bushy tail. He was so proud of it that he combed it all the time. He also sang about it at every dance. Rabbit had a small tail and he was jealous of Possum.

Rabbit brought news to all the animals that there would be a special dance soon. When Rabbit stopped at Possum's place, Possum asked for a special seat at the dance. "I have such a beautiful tail," he said, "that I should sit where all can see me."

Rabbit agreed. He told Possum that he would even send someone to dress up his tail for the dance. This pleased Possum.

Then Rabbit went to Cricket. The Rabbit told Cricket to go to the Possum before the dance. Rabbit told Cricket just how to cut Possum's tail.

When Cricket went to help Possum get his tail ready, Possum welcomed him proudly. Possum lay down and closed his eyes.

Cricket combed the tail and wrapped a red string around it to keep it smooth until the dance. But as he wound the string, he cut off the hair—and Possum never knew it.

At the dance that night, Possum sat in his special seat. When his turn came, Possum took off the red string and strode to the middle of the floor. He began to sing, "See my beautiful tail."

All the animals shouted, and Possum danced. He sang, "See the wonderful colors of it." And all the animals shouted again. "See how fine the fur is."

The animals all laughed so long, Possum wondered why. He finally looked at his tail and saw that no hair was left on it. It was as bare as the tail of Lizard. He was so surprised and ashamed he rolled over on the ground—just as he does today when he is surprised.

Native American tale retold by Dawn Purney

How did I read?	How can I do better?
☺ ☺ ☺	

Odd Word Out

1. Circle the word in each group that does not belong.
Then write a category for the words that do belong
together, such as "things that are alive."

Category

jealous proud happy singing _____

eyes tail comb hair _____

proud dance shout laugh _____

rabbit possum tail lizard _____

Find Synonyms

2. Find a word in the story that means the same as each word below.

center _____

greeted _____

yelled _____

embarrassed _____

Find Antonyms

3. Now find a word in the story that means the opposite of each word below.

started _____

opened _____

stand _____

Today

Yesterday is gone.
Tomorrow has not yet come.
We have only today.
Let us begin.

Mother Teresa

Life itself cannot give you joy
Unless you really will it.
Life just gives you time and space
And it's up to you to fill it.

Chinese Proverb

When planning for a year, plant corn.
When planning for a decade, plant trees.
When planning for life, train and educate people.

Chinese Proverb

How did I read?	How can I do better?

Nouns and Verbs

1. Some words in these three selections can be used as nouns or verbs. Read the pairs of sentences below. Then write **noun** or **verb** to show how each underlined word is used.

I have no <u>time</u> to play games today.   _____

I will <u>time</u> the race.   _____

You should <u>space</u> the chairs one foot apart. _____

The box was just taking up <u>space</u>.   _____

I will <u>plant</u> those flowers by the sidewalk. _____

Which <u>plant</u> did you water?   _____

Compare Quotations

2. Which selection on page 68 means almost the same as the quotation below? Explain how the quotation is like the selection.

> **Never leave that till tomorrow which you can do today.**
> *-Benjamin Franklin*

_____

_____

_____

Excellence

We are what we repeatedly do.
Excellence, then, is not an act, but a habit.

Aristotle

If you don't want others to know what you have done,
Better not have done it in the first place.

Chinese Proverb

Be not afraid of growing slowly,
be afraid only of standing still.

Chinese Proverb

Teachers open the door.
You enter by yourself.

Chinese Proverb

How did I read?	How can I do better?
☺ ☺ ☺	

Add Suffixes

1. Choose the correct suffix from the box and add it to the word. Write your new word in the sentence. Use each suffix once.

-less	-ful	-ing	-ness	-ship	-ly	-ed

work   They were _____ hard.

open   She _____ the door.

care   Be _____ what you wish for!

care   Do not be _____ with those scissors!

quick   He _____ made his choice.

kind   I appreciate your _____ in waiting for me.

friend   A _____ can last your whole lifetime.

Explain the Proverbs

2. Read the quotation from Aristotle. Explain what he meant in your own words.

_____

3. Read the Chinese proverb about teachers. What does this tell students?

_____

_____

Broccoli and Brussels Sprouts

Broccoli and Brussels sprouts
are my favorite foods, no doubt;
If only you could see my grin
when dad says that's what's for din.

My brother Rob and sister Kate
would rather have an empty plate.
They'd rather whine and frown and pout
than eat a single Brussels sprout!

One day I hope they'll love the taste
and no more send a sprout to waste.
Perhaps one day they'll learn to talk
about the tasty broccoli stalk.

But for now I'll sit and wait,
and savor the veggies on my plate.
For when they love the stuff like me,
I'll have to split my greens in three!

Laura Portalupi

How did I read?	How can I do better?
☹	

Odd Word Out

1. Circle the word in each group that does not rhyme.

sprout   scout   shoot   doubt   trout

Kate   wait   bait   that   plate

taste   past   paste   waste   haste

blank   chalk   talk   walk   stalk

Change the Word

2. Write a word that rhymes with **plate** for each definition.

what you do on ice   _____

a door in a fence   _____

Iowa, Texas, and Oregon   _____

a certain day on a calendar   _____

Write Your Own Poem

3. Choose a food that you love or hate. Then think of words that rhyme with that food.

The food: _____

Words that rhyme with the food: _____

_____

To Belize

I'm taking an airplane to Belize.
In my bag I'm packing an apple,
A book, a cup, a dress, earmuffs, and fleas.

I'm taking an airplane to Belize.
In my bag I'm packing gloves,
A hat, ink, a jump rope, and my keys.

I'm taking an airplane to Belize.
In my bag I'm packing a lamp,
Markers, noodles, oranges, and peas.

I'm taking an airplane to Belize.
In my bag I'm packing a quarter,
A ring, a surfboard, a toothbrush, and an umbrella for the breeze.

I'm taking an airplane to Belize.
In my bag I'm packing a vase,
A wig, a xylophone, a yo-yo, and zucchinis.

Laura Portalupi

How did I read?	How can I do better?

Compound Words

1. Use the clues to choose a word to add to each word
below to make the compound word.

a place where planes land   air_____

small, round pieces of cloth or fur   ear_____

a piece of jewelry   ear_____

for riding on waves   _____board

for cleaning teeth   tooth_____

sometimes tastes like mint   tooth_____

a way to travel   air_____

Finish the Group

2. Write a word from the poem to fit in each group below.

pasta   spaghetti   _____

nickel   penny   _____

truck   car   _____

necklace   bracelet   _____

mosquitoes   spiders   _____

crayons   chalk   _____

from Little Women

Little Women *is the story of the March family, who lived in New England around the time of the Civil War. In this selection Jo March is visiting her neighbor, Laurie, who must stay in the house because he's sick.*

Up went a handful of snow. The head turned at once, showing a face which lost its listless look in a minute, as the big eyes brightened and the mouth began to smile. Jo nodded and laughed and flourished her broom, as she called out, "How do you do? Are you sick?" Laurie opened the window and croaked out as hoarsely as a raven, "Better, thank you. I've had a horrible cold and been shut up a week."

"I'm sorry. What do you amuse yourself with?"

"Nothing. It's dull as tombs up here."

"Don't you read?"

"Not much. They won't let me."

"Can't somebody read to you?"

"Grandpa does, sometimes; but my books don't interest him and I hate to ask Brooke all the time."

"Have someone come and see you, then."

"There isn't anyone I'd like to see. Boys make such a row, and my head is weak."

"Isn't there some nice girl who'd read and amuse you? Girls are quiet and they like to play nurse."

"Don't know any."

"You know us," began Jo, then laughed and stopped.

"So I do! Will you come, please?" cried Laurie.

"I'm not nice and quiet, but I'll come if Mother will let me. I'll go ask her. Shut that window, like a good boy, and wait till I come."

Louisa May Alcott

How did I read?	How can I do better?

Fluency First!

Answer Like Laurie

1. Answer these questions as Laurie would.

How long have you been sick? _____

Has it been fun being home? _____

Has anyone read to you? _____

Who do you want to visit you? _____

Comparing

2. Complete the Venn diagram to compare things Laurie does when he is sick to things that you do.

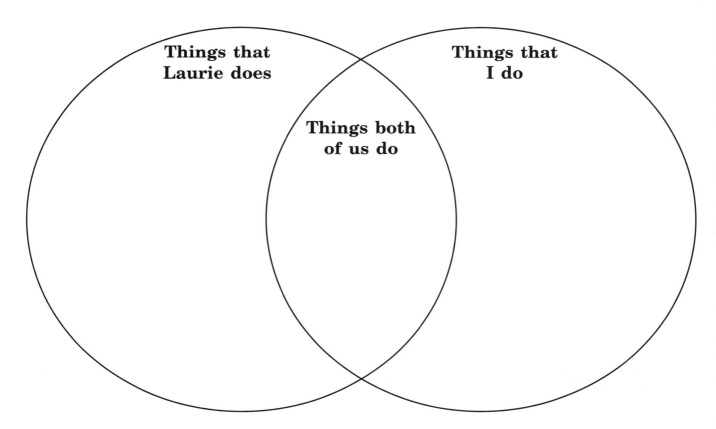

Things that
Laurie does

Things that
I do

Things both
of us do

from Little Women

Laurie's doctor has come to visit, so Jo is left alone in the library.

She was standing before a fine portrait of old Mr. Laurence when the door opened again. She was saying softly to herself, "He isn't as handsome as my grandfather, but I think I could like him."

"Thank you, ma'am," said a gruff voice behind her; and there, to her great dismay, stood old Mr. Laurence.

For a minute, a wild desire to run away possessed Jo. But that would be cowardly, so she resolved to stay and get out of the scrape as best she could.

The voice was gruffer than ever, as the old gentleman said, "So you don't think me quite as handsome as your grandfather?"

"Not quite, sir."

"But you like me in spite of it?"

"Yes, I do, sir."

That answer pleased the old gentleman; he gave a short laugh and shook hands with her. "You've got your grandfather's spirit," he said. "He was a fine man, my dear. But what's better, he was a brave and honest one, and I was proud to be his friend."

"Thank you, sir," said Jo, relieved.

Louisa May Alcott

How did I read?	How can I do better?

Jo's Surprise

1. Why did Jo suddenly want to run away?

_____

_____

2. Why does she decide to stay?

_____

_____

3. What did Mr. Laurence think about Jo's grandfather?

_____

Talking Portrait

4. Draw a portrait of Mr. Laurence. Use a speech bubble to fill in the words he would say to describe who he is.

Rainy Day

Rainy day, rainy day, I like it;
My mother will come here with my umbrella,
Pitch pitch, chap chap, run run run!

Bag on my shoulder, I follow my mother;
A bell is ringing somewhere,
Pitch pitch, chap chap, run run run!

Oh oh, that girl is dripping wet;
She is crying under the willow,
Pitch pitch, chap chap, run run run!

Mother, mother, I'll lend my umbrella;
"Hi girl, use this umbrella,"
Pitch pitch, chap chap, run run run!

I am all right, don't worry,
Mother will take me in her big umbrella,
Pitch pitch, chap chap, run run run!

Japanese song

How did I read?	How can I do better?

Action Words

1. Words that name an action are called verbs. Write sentences using each of these action words from the poem.

follow

_____

lend

_____

use

_____

worry

_____

take

_____

Explain the Sound

2. Each verse of the poem ends with the words, "Pitch pitch, chap chap, run run run!" Explain in your own words what sound these words stand for.

_____

_____

from Toboggan

Down from the hills and over the snow
Swift as a meteor's flash we go,
   Toboggan! Toboggan! Toboggan!
Down from the hills with our senses lost,
Jealous of cheeks that are kissed by the frost,
   Toboggan! Toboggan! Toboggan!

With snow piled high on housetop and hill,
Over frozen rivulet, river, and rill,
Clad in her jacket of sealskin and fur,
Down from the hills I'm sliding with her,
   Toboggan! Toboggan! Toboggan!

Down from the hills, what an awful speed!
As if on the back of a frightened steed,
   Toboggan! Toboggan! Toboggan!
Down from the hills at the rise of the moon,
Merrily singing the toboggan tune,
   "Toboggan! Toboggan! Toboggan!"

Down from the hills like an arrow we fly,
Or a comet that whizzes along through the sky;
Down from the hills! Oh, isn't it grand!
Clasping your best winter friend by the hand,
   Toboggan! Toboggan! Toboggan!

Benjamin Franklin King, Jr.

How did I read?	How can I do better?
☺ ☺ ☹	

In Other Words

1. Using your own words, explain what these phrases
   from the poem mean.

   swift as a meteor's flash _____

   what an awful speed! _____

   like an arrow we fly _____

   isn't it grand! _____

   your best winter friend _____

Complete the Rhyme

2. Write a word to finish each rhyme.

   Over the ground, we're moving so fast,

   the wind whistles by as we go _____.

   The snow is so bright, it goes crackle and crunch,

   I hold out my mittens and catch a big _____.

   Our fingers are frozen, our toes are so cold,

   but we're feeling brave and ever so _____.

from Charlotte's Web

Here's a description of Wilbur the Pig's first taste of freedom.

One afternoon in June, when Wilbur was almost two months old, he wandered out into his small yard....

"There's never anything to do out here," he thought.... "When I'm out here," he said, "there's no place to go but in. When I'm indoors, there's no place to go but out in the yard."

"That's where you're wrong, my friend, my friend," said a voice. Wilbur...saw the goose standing there. "You don't have to stay in that dirty-little dirty-little dirty-little yard," said the goose, who talked rather fast. "One of the boards is loose. Push on it, push-push-push on it, and it will come out!"...

Wilbur walked up to the fence.... He put his head down, shut his eyes, and pushed. The board gave way. In a minute...[he] was standing in the long grass outside his yard. The goose chuckled.

"How does it feel to be free?" she asked.

"I like it," said Wilbur.... "Where do you think I'd better go?"

"Anywhere you like, anywhere you like," said the goose. "...Go down to the garden, dig up the radishes!... Eat grass! Look for corn! Look for oats! Run all over! Skip and dance, jump and prance!... The world is a wonderful place when you're young."

"I can see that," replied Wilbur. He gave a jump in the air, twirled, ran a few steps, stopped, looked all around, sniffed the smells of the afternoon, and then set off walking down through the orchard.

E. B. White

How did I read?	How can I do better?
☺ ☺ ☹	

Imagining Wilbur

1. What are some things that the goose said Wilbur could do if he were free? List some below and draw a picture to go with one.

_____

_____

_____

_____

_____

_____

Make New Words

2. Use the letters in the word **smell** to create new words. Continue to change one letter each time to make a new word.

This is what we do when we use letters to make words. _____

Here is a word for when water pours onto the floor. _____

This word means "not moving." _____

This word is the name of where a horse lives. _____

This word describes crusty, old bread. _____

from Charlotte's Web

Here's an excerpt from the scene where Wilbur meets Charlotte for the first time.

"Salutations," said the voice.

Wilbur jumped to his feet. "Salu—what?"

"Salutations!" repeated the voice.

"What are they, and where are you?" screamed Wilbur. "Please, please, tell me where you are. And what are salutations?"

"Salutations are greetings," said the voice. "When I say 'salutations,' it's just my fancy way of saying hello or good morning. Actually, it's a silly expression, and I am surprised that I used it at all. As for my whereabouts, that's easy. Look up here in the corner of the doorway! Here I am. Look, I'm waving!"

At last Wilbur saw the creature that had spoken to him in such a kindly way. Stretched across the upper part of the doorway was a big spider web, and hanging from the top of the web, head down, was a large grey spider.

E. B. White

How did I read?	How can I do better?
☹	

Word Endings

1. Nouns often end in **-ion**. Find and write the words in the selection that end in **-ion** or **-ions**.

   _____   _____

2. Read the clues and write the **-ion** word from the box that fits. Hint: You will not use all the words.

lotion   station   question   action   nation   motion

   another name for a country   _____

   a cream for making skin soft   _____

   something you ask   _____

   a place where a train or bus stops   _____

Write Similar Phrases

3. Look at this phrase from the selection. It describes where Charlotte is. On the lines below, write three phrases of your own replacing the underlined words with other words.

   Example: **here in the <u>corner</u> of the <u>doorway</u>**

   here in the _____ of the _____

   here in the _____ of the _____

   here in the _____ of the _____

Sounder's Voice

Sounder is the story of an African American family and their dog. Here is a description of Sounder's amazing voice.

Sounder's voice…came out of the great chest cavity and broad jaws as though it had bounced off the walls of a cave. It mellowed into half-echo before it touched the air.… Each bark bounced from slope to slope in the foothills like a rubber ball. But it was not an ordinary bark. It filled up the night and made music as though the branches of all the trees were being pulled across silver strings.

A stranger hearing Sounder's…bark suddenly fill the night might have thought there were six dogs at the foot of one tree. But all over the countryside, neighbors, leaning against slanting porch posts or standing in open cabin doorways and listening, knew that it was Sounder.

William H. Armstrong

How did I read?	How can I do better?
☺ ☺ ☺	

Word Endings

1. On the lines below, write short sentences using the six words
in the selection that end with **-ing**.

_____

_____

_____

_____

_____

_____

Compounds

2. Read the words from the selection. Circle the compound words.

countryside	description	neighbor	foothills
ordinary	doorways	cabin	suddenly

Describe It

3. Describe in your own words the sound of Sounder's voice.

_____

_____

from How to Tell the Wild Animals

If ever you should go by chance
To Jungles in the East;
And if there should to you advance
A large and tawny beast,
If he roars at you as you're dyin'
You'll know it is the Asian Lion.

Or if some time when roaming round,
A noble wild beast greets you,
With black stripes on a yellow ground,
Just notice if he eats you.
This simple rule may help you learn
The Bengal Tiger to discern.

If strolling forth, a beast you view,
Whose hide with spots is peppered,
As soon as he has lept on you,
You'll know it is the Leopard.
'Twill do no good to roar with pain,
He'll only lep and lep again.

If when you're walking round your yard,
You meet a creature there,
Who hugs you very, very hard,
Be sure it is the Bear.
If you have any doubt, I guess
He'll give you just one more caress.

Carolyn Wells

How did I read?	How can I do better?

Word Endings

1. Two sets of rhyming words from the first verse are written below. Next to them, write two more words that rhyme with them.

chance   advance   _____   _____

East   beast   _____   _____

2. Other rhyming words from the poem are written below. On the lines following them, write two more words that rhyme.

round   ground   _____   _____

learn   discern   _____   _____

guess   caress   _____   _____

Picture This!

3. In the space below, draw one of the animals in the poem.

Irish Well Wishes

Here's to health, peace and prosperity. May the flower of love never be nipped by the frost of disappointment, nor shadow of grief fall among your family and friends.

May you be poor in misfortune, rich in blessings, slow to make enemies and quick to make friends. And may you know nothing but happiness from this day forward.

May you have warm words on a cold evening, a full moon on a dark night, and a smooth road all the way to your door.

Authors unknown

How did I read?	How can I do better?
☺ ☺ ☺	

Double Vowels

1. Write the words in the selection that have a **double o** letter combination (**oo**).

_____   _____

_____   _____

2. Write six more words with the **double o** letter combination.

_____   _____

_____   _____

_____   _____

Write Your Own

3. Write your own well wishes by filling in the blanks below.

May you be poor in _____

and rich in _____.

May you have _____,

_____,

and _____.

A Joke

Did you hear about the teacher who was helping one of her kindergarten students put on his boots? He asked for help, and she could see why he needed it.

Even with her pulling and him pushing, the little boots still didn't want to go on. Finally, when the second boot was on, she had worked up a sweat.

She almost cried when the little boy said, "Teacher, they're on the wrong feet."

She looked and sure enough, they were. It wasn't any easier pulling the boots off than it was putting them on. They worked to get the boots back on—this time on the right feet.

He then announced, "These aren't my boots."

Once again she struggled to help him pull the boots off his little feet. As soon as they got the boots off, he said, "They're my brother's boots. My mom made me wear 'em."

Now she didn't know if she should laugh or cry. But, she mustered up the grace and courage she had left to wrestle the boots on his feet again. Helping him into his coat, she asked, "Now, where are your mittens?" He said, "I stuffed 'em in the toes of my boots."

Author unknown

How did I read?	How can I do better?
☺ ☺ ☹	

Double Letters

1. Look in the selection for words with double letters.
Can you find all 18? Write them on the lines below.

_____   _____

_____   _____

_____   _____

_____   _____

_____   _____

_____   _____

_____   _____

Recognizing Sequence

2. Read the sentences below. Number them in the order in which
they happen in the selection.

_____ Student tells teacher the boots are not his.

_____ Teacher asks where the boy's mittens are.

_____ Teacher puts boots on the wrong feet.

_____ Student asks teacher for help with his boots.

_____ Boy says the boots belong to his brother.

Paul Revere's Ride

Listen, my children, and you shall hear

Of the midnight ride of Paul Revere,

On the eighteenth of April, in Seventy-five;

Hardly a man is now alive

Who remembers that famous day and year.

He said to his friend, "If the British march

By land or sea from the town to-night,

Hang a lantern aloft in the belfry-arch

Of the North Church tower as a signal light,—

One, if by land, and two, if by sea;

And I on the opposite shore will be,

Ready to ride and spread the alarm

Through every Middlesex village and farm,

For the country folk to be up and to arm."

Henry W. Longfellow

How did I read?	How can I do better?
☺ ☺ ☹	

Word Endings

1. Two sets of rhyming words from the first verse are written below. Next to them, write two more words that rhyme with them.

hear   year   _____   _____

five   alive   _____   _____

2. Other rhyming words from the poem are written below. On the lines that follow them, write two more words that rhyme.

sea   be   _____   _____

light   night   _____   _____

Write Similar Phrases

3. Look at the phrases below from the selection. On the lines below, rewrite these phrases into modern language.

Hang a lantern aloft

_____

Ready to ride and spread the alarm

_____

If the British march
By land or sea from the town to-night

_____

_____

The Dream Keeper

Bring me all of your dreams,
You dreamer,
Bring me all your
Heart melodies
That I may wrap them
In a blue cloud-cloth
Away from the too-rough fingers
Of the world.

Langston Hughes

How did I read?	How can I do better?

Figures of Speech

1. Langston Hughes uses language to create pictures and express feelings in the poem. Write what you think the poet means by the following phrases:

   What are "heart melodies"?

   _____

   Why does the Dream Keeper "...wrap them in a blue cloud-cloth"?

   _____

   What does "...too-rough fingers of the world" mean?

   _____

What Do You See?

2. Imagine that The Dream Keeper is a person. What does The Dream Keeper look like? How would the dreams be collected? Draw the picture that the poem paints in your mind.

What Is the United States Constitution?

The people of the United States joined together in 1789 to create a new government to rule the land and its people. They wrote a Constitution, or set of laws, that the new government would follow. These laws were:

- make sure the country is peaceful,
- protect the people's health and happiness,
- create a fair legal system, and
- defend the country's people and their future children.

Fill in the Blanks

1. Use words from the selection to fill in the blanks.

    The new government would rule the land and the _____.

    The Constitution is a set of _____.

    The Constitution does all these:

    - makes sure the country is _____.

    - protects people's _____ and happiness.

    - creates a _____ legal system.

    - _____ the country's people.

What Does It Mean?

2. Choose one of the laws in the selection and explain how you think the government does it, or could do it.

    _____

    _____

    _____

    _____

    _____

    _____

What Is the Bill of Rights?

The Bill of Rights is a list of people's rights defended by the government. The Bill of Rights is the first ten amendments to the U.S. Constitution. The First Amendment is one of the most important. It guarantees all Americans the freedom to talk about their ideas, the freedom of the press to report, and the freedom to come together with other people as a group. It also protects our right to choose a religion or to choose not to worship. The First Amendment also protects the right of citizens to demand changes in their government.

How did I read?	How can I do better?
☺ ☺ ☺	

Find the Word

1. Find the word from the selection
to match each definition.

the ability to make choices _____

the people and laws that run a country _____

changes to laws _____

Multiple Meaning Words

2. Use the correct word from the box in each sentence.
Use each word twice.

right	press	Bill

When you get to the corner, turn _____.

A former president was named _____ Clinton.

To shut the door, _____ hard.

Everyone has the _____ to make their own choices.

Only reporters and other members of the _____ are allowed in.

The first ten amendments are called the _____ of Rights.

adapted from Heidi

Heidi is an orphan girl who is being taken by her Aunt Dete, who can no longer care for her, to her grandfather's hut in the Alps. Here is a description of Heidi and Aunt Dete's trip up the mountain.

From the old village of Mayenfeld, a footpath winds through green meadows to the foot of the mountains, which on this side looks down upon the valley below. The climber has not gone far before he begins to inhale the fragrance of the short grass, for the way is steep and leads directly up.

On a clear sunny morning in June two figures might be seen climbing the narrow mountain path; one, a tall strong-looking girl, the other a child, whose little cheeks were aglow and crimson. This was hardly to be wondered at, for in spite of the hot June sun the child was clothed as if to keep off the bitterest frost. She did not look more than five years old. She had apparently two, if not three dresses, one above the other, and over these a thick red woolen shawl wound round about her, so that the little body presented a shapeless appearance. With its small feet in thick, nailed mountain-shoes, it slowly plodded its way up in the heat.

Johanna Spyri

How did I read?	How can I do better?

Describing Words

1. List the describing words from the selection on the lines.

_____   _____

_____   _____

_____   _____

_____   _____

_____   _____

Picture This

2. Draw a picture of the setting the author describes.

adapted from Heidi

In this scene from the book Heidi, *by Johanna Spyri, Heidi and her Grandfather start to get to know each other.*

As soon as Dete had disappeared the old man went back to his bench, and there he remained seated, staring on the ground without uttering a sound. Heidi was enjoying herself in her new surroundings. She looked about till she found a shed, built against the hut, where the goats were kept. She peeped in, and saw it was empty.

She continued her search and came to the fir trees behind the hut. A strong breeze was blowing through them, and there was a rushing and roaring in their topmost branches. Heidi stood still and listened. The sound growing fainter, she went on again, to the farther corner of the hut, and so round to where her grandfather was sitting.

Seeing that he was in exactly the same position as when she left him, she went and placed herself in front of the old man, and putting her hands behind her back, stood and gazed at him.

Her grandfather looked up, and as she continued standing there without moving, "What is it you want?" he asked.

"I want to see what you have inside the house," said Heidi.

Johanna Spyri

How did I read?	How can I do better?
☺ ☺ ☺	

Compound Words

1. Circle the compound words found in the story.

grandfather	continued	disappeared	uttering
search	peeped	herself	blowing
exactly	against	empty	topmost
bench	inside	enjoying	rushing

Character Sketch

2. Pretend that you are Heidi and that you are writing
a letter to a friend about your grandfather. What would
you tell your friend about him?

_____

_____

_____

_____

_____

_____

The Real Princess

There was once a prince who wished to marry a real princess. He had traveled all over the world in hopes of finding such a lady, but there was always something wrong. He found plenty of princesses, but he could not decide if they were real princesses. At last he returned to his palace quite cast down, because he wished so much to have a real princess for his wife.

All at once there was heard a violent knocking at the door, and the old king, the prince's father, went out himself to open it. It was a princess who was standing outside the door. What with the rain and the wind, the water trickled down from her hair, and her clothes clung to her body. She said she was a real princess.

"Ah! we shall soon see that!" thought the old queen-mother, who went quietly into the bedroom, took all the bed-clothes off the bed, and put three little peas on the bedstead. She then laid twenty mattresses one upon another over the three peas, and put twenty feather beds over the mattresses. Upon this bed the princess was to pass the night.

The next morning she was asked how she had slept. "Oh, very badly indeed!" she replied. "I do not know what was in my bed, but I had something hard under me, and am all over black and blue."

Now it was plain that the lady must be a real princess, since she had been able to feel the three little peas through the twenty mattresses and twenty feather beds. None but a real princess could have had such a delicate sense of feeling.

The prince made her his wife; being now convinced that he had found a real princess. The three peas were however put into the cabinet of curiosities, where they are still to be seen, provided they are not lost.

Hans Christian Andersen

How did I read?	How can I do better?
☺ ☺ ☹	

A Real Princess

1. Why was it hard to believe at first that the girl at
the door was a real princess?

_____

2. What was the Queen's plan to test the girl?

_____

3. What convinced everyone that the girl was a real princess?

_____

Illustrate the Story

4. Draw a picture of some part of the story. Write a
sentence under your picture.

```



```

_____

The Crow and the Pitcher

A crow, half-dead with thirst, came upon a pitcher which had once been full of water; but when the crow put its beak into the mouth of the pitcher he found that only very little water was left in it, and that he could not reach far enough down to get at it. He tried, and he tried, but at last had to give up in despair.

Then a thought came to him, and he took a pebble and dropped it into the pitcher. Then he took another pebble and dropped it into the pitcher. Then he took another pebble and dropped that into the pitcher. Then he took another pebble and dropped that into the pitcher. Then he took another pebble and dropped that into the pitcher. Then he took another pebble and dropped that into the pitcher.

At last, at last, he saw the water mount up near him, and after casting in a few more pebbles he was able to quench his thirst and save his life.

Little by little does the trick.

Aesop

How did I read?	How can I do better?
☺ ☺ ☹	

Sorting by Syllables

1. Sometimes words with double consonants have two syllables like: **bub/ble**. And sometimes they have one, like **tripped**.
Sort the following words from the selection to complete the chart.

full	little	dropped	pebble

Words with one syllable	Words with two syllables
_____	_____
_____	_____

Retell the Story

2. Pretend that you are retelling the fable to a friend.
Write a short summary of what happens in the fable.

_____

_____

_____

_____

_____

The Mess

I feel a bit uptight.
I feel a little stress.
Everything I try to do
Ends up in a mess.

When I went to feed the horses
I had a bunch of hay
But I left the barn door open
And the horses ran away.

For the pigs I had a bucket
That was filled up to the top,
But I stumbled on a piggy
And I fell into the slop.

The cow spilled half the milk,
The rabbit scratched my nose,
The duck all up and flew away,
The goat ate half my clothes.

"I'm ready, Gramps," I smiled and said,
"I need another chore."
But then my Grandpa shouted back,
"Don't help me anymore!"

That's why I'm so uptight.
That's why I'm full of stress.
Everything I try to do
Ends up in a mess.

Brod Bagert

How did I read?	How can I do better?

Digraphs

1. The letter **h** can be combined with other letters to make one sound. Find the words with letter **h** combinations in the poem. Then write more words with these combinations.

th	**wh**	**gh**

tch	**ch**	**sh**

Puppy Disobedience

Puppy, no. That's Daddy's shoe.
Puppy, puppy, please don't chew.
Puppy, don't! That's even worse—
Never chew on Mama's purse!

Puppy, that's my sister's doll,
That could be the worst of all.
My sister loves that doll the most—
She'd turn you into puppy-toast.

Puppy, please don't try to hide,
It's time for you to go outside.
Puppy, no! Don't try to flee—
Don't try to run away from me.

I know now why my parents raved
All those times I misbehaved!
I know because it's plain to see
My puppy acts a lot like me.

Brod Bagert

How did I read?	How can I do better?
☺ ☺ ☹	

Long Vowels

1. Write eight words from the selection that contain the **long e** vowel sound. Circle the letter or letters that make the **long e** sound.

_____   _____

_____   _____

_____   _____

_____   _____

What's the Problem?

2. List three bad things the puppy does.

_____

_____

_____

Write About

3. The speaker in the poem probably does not chew on shoes, so what does this phrase "My puppy acts a lot like me" mean?

_____

_____

_____

from The Secret Garden

In this passage, Mary uses a key she has found to open the door to a secret garden.

She put her hands under the leaves and began to pull and push them aside. Thick as the ivy hung, it nearly all was a loose and swinging curtain, though some had crept over wood and iron. Mary's heart began to thump and her hands to shake a little in her delight and excitement.... What was this under her hands which was square and made of iron and which her fingers found a hole in?

It was the lock of the door which had been closed ten years and she put her hand in her pocket, drew out the key and found it fitted the keyhole. She put the key in and turned it. It took two hands to do it, but it did turn.... She took another long breath, because she could not help it, and she held back the swinging curtain of ivy and pushed back the door which opened slowly—slowly.

Then she slipped through it, and shut it behind her, and stood with her back against it, looking about her and breathing quite fast with excitement, and wonder, and delight.

She was standing inside the secret garden.

Frances Hodgson Burnett

How did I read?	How can I do better?
☺ ☺ ☹	

How Does She Do That?

1. Underline the words from the selection that tell how the door opened.

   She took another long breath, because she could not help it, and she held back the swinging curtain of ivy and pushed back the door which opened slowly—slowly.

2. Many words that tell how something was done end with **-ly**
   Write more words you know that end in **-ly** that tell how
   something can be done.

   _____   _____

   _____   _____

How Does Mary Feel?

3. How do you think Mary feels in this selection? In the diagram
   below, copy words and phrases from the selection that tell how
   Mary feels.

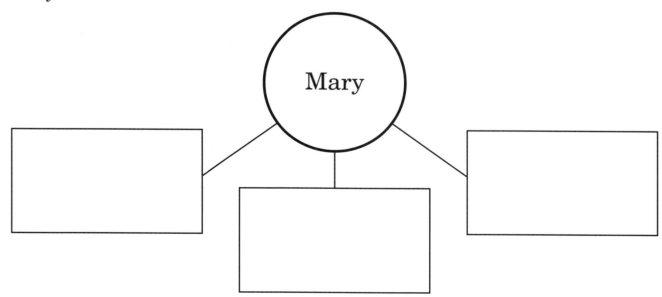

from The Secret Garden

Here, Mary describes the Secret Garden.

It was the sweetest, most mysterious-looking place anyone could imagine. The high walls which shut it in were covered with the leafless stems of climbing roses which were so thick that they were matted together.... All the ground was covered with grass of a wintry brown and out of it grew clumps of bushes which were surely rosebushes if they were alive.

There were numbers of standard roses which had so spread their branches that they were like little trees. There were other trees in the garden, and one of the things which made the place look strangest and loveliest was that climbing roses had run all over them and swung down long tendrils which made light, swaying curtains, and here and there they had caught at each other or at a far-reaching branch and had crept from one tree to another and made lovely bridges of themselves.

Frances Hodgson Burnett

How did I read?	How can I do better?
☺ ☹	

Finding the Right Word

1. This selection contains several words that end in **-est**. Find the words and write them below in the first column. Then, in the second column, write the word that the **-est** word describes. The first one is done for you.

Word that end with <u>-est</u>	What the word describes
sweetest	garden

Picture It

2. Draw a picture of Mary in the Secret Garden.

from The Life of Christopher Columbus

Christopher Columbus was a famous explorer. He was one of the first Europeans to visit the land we now call America. Here, the author tells us about Columbus and his idea that the earth was round. At the time, many people thought the earth was flat.

We must not [think] that the idea of the roundness of the earth was invented by Columbus. Although there were other [ideas] about its shape, many intelligent men... understood that the earth was a globe.

There is a very funny story...in which a traveler [goes], mostly on foot, through all the countries of Asia, but finally [returns] to Norway, his home. In his farthest eastern [travels], he hears some people calling their cattle by a peculiar cry, which he had never heard before.

After he returned home, it was necessary for him to take a day's journey westward to look after some cattle he had lost. Finding these cattle, he also heard the same cry...which he had heard in the extreme East. [He] now learned, for the first time, that he had gone round the world on foot, to turn and come back by the same route, when he was only a day's journey from home.

Columbus [knew] such stories...which almost made him know that the world was round. The difficulty was to persuade other people that, because of this roundness, it would be possible to [travel to] Asia by sailing to the West.

Edward Everett Hale

How did I read?	How can I do better?
☺ ☺ ☺	

Looking at Word Endings

1. Add **-ness** to each of the words below to make a new word.

    fat   _____

    fair   _____

    dry   _____

    bright   _____

    dark   _____

2. Complete each of these sentences with a new word from above.

    Almost no plants could grow because of the _____

    in the desert.

    When the moon went behind a cloud, the _____

    of the forest was amazing.

    The _____ of the chickens made the fox very hungry.

    The sun's _____ made it hard to see anything.

    Everyone praised the _____ of the wise king's decision.

from The Life of Christopher Columbus

To get to the New World, explorers from Europe had to cross the Atlantic Ocean. Here, we find out how Columbus planned to pay for his journey.

While there were so many suggestions made that it would be possible to cross the Atlantic [Ocean], there was one man who [was] determined to do this. This man was Christopher Columbus. But he knew well that he could not do it alone.

He must have money enough for an expedition, he must [find] crews for that expedition, and he must [be in charge of] those crews when they should arrive in the Indies. In our times such adventures have been [completed] by [traders], but in those times no one thought of doing any such thing without the direct assistance and support of some monarch.

Edward Everett Hale

How did I read?	How can I do better?
☺ ☺ ☹	

Now and Then

1. Look at the sentence from the selection. Notice how
the underlined parts contrast the present with the past.

> <u>In our times</u>, such adventures have been [completed] by [traders],
> <u>but in those times</u> no one thought of doing any such thing without
> the direct assistance and support of some monarch.

Use these phrases to compare the present with the past.
The first one is done for you.

In our times **we drove cars** , but in those times **they rode horses** .

In our times _____, but in those times _____.

In our times _____, but in those times _____.

In our times _____, but in those times _____.

In our times _____, but in those times _____.

In our times _____, but in those times _____.

I Can't Hear You, K

2. Write the word in the selection with a **silent k** at the beginning.
Then write three more words that begin with a **silent k**.

_____   _____

_____   _____

from Songs of Innocence and Experience

Sound the flute!
Now it's mute!
Birds delight,
Day and night,
Nightingale,
In the dale,
Lark in sky,
Merrily,
Merrily, merrily to welcome in the year.

Little boy,
Full of joy;
Little girl,
Sweet and small;
[Rooster] does crow,
So do you;
Merry voice,
Infant noise;
Merrily, merrily to welcome in the year.

Little lamb,
Here I am;
Come and lick
My white neck;
Let me pull
Your soft wool;
Let me kiss
Your soft face;
Merrily, merrily we welcome in the year.

William Blake

<table>
<tr><td>How did I read?</td><td>How can I do better?</td></tr>
<tr><td>☺ ☺ ☺</td><td></td></tr>
</table>

Antonyms

1. Write words from the poem that have opposite meanings.

day   _____

black   _____

big   _____

hard   _____

Adjectives

2. List words from the poem that describe the characters.

boy   _____

lamb   _____

girl   _____

Categorize Words

3. Write words from the poem that name birds.

_____

_____

_____

from The Song of Hiawatha

Hiawatha is a legendary American Indian hero. This excerpt from a famous poem tells about the place where Hiawatha's people live.

By the shore of Gitche Gumee,
By the shining Big-Sea-Water,
At the doorway of his wigwam,
In the pleasant Summer morning,
Hiawatha stood and waited.
All the air was full of freshness,
All the earth was bright and joyous,
And before him, through the sunshine,
Westward toward the neighboring forest
Passed in golden swarms the Ahmo,
Passed the bees, the honey-makers,
Burning, singing in the sunshine.

Henry Wadsworth Longfellow

How did I read?	How can I do better?
☺ ☺ ☺	

Compound Words

1. Write the two words that make up each compound word from
the selection. Then write a definition for the compound word.

- doorway _____   _____

_____

- sunshine _____   _____

_____

- westward _____   _____

_____

Descriptive Words

2. Find and list words that describe air.

_____

3. Find and list words that describe earth.

_____

4. Find and list words that describe water.

_____

from Space Songs

Space blazes with jewels,
a shimmering ice
of billions of diamonds
dazzles
the Milky Way:
Jupiter, a giant agate,
Uranus, a ball of jade,
Pluto, a luminescent pearl,
Saturn, a halo of rings,
A slice
of moon, a crescent brooch.
Bright rubies splay
Antares
in this
midnight
masquerade.

Myra Cohn Livingston

<table>
<tr><td>How did I read?</td><td>How can I do better?</td></tr>
<tr><td> ☺ ☺ ☺</td><td></td></tr>
</table>

Categorize Words

1. Write each word from the poem to complete the chart.

| rubies | Milky Way | Jupiter | agate | rings |
| Saturn | jade | Pluto | diamonds | brooch |

Jewels	Jewelry	Object in Space
_____	_____	_____
_____	_____	_____
_____	_____	_____
_____	_____	_____
_____	_____	_____

2. Now go back and add a word in each category. The word can be from the poem or another word that fits.

How Did You Know?

3. Choose one category above. Explain how you knew the words fit in the category.

_____

_____

_____

Who is Maya Angelou?

Maya Angelou is a poet, teacher, historian, author, actress, and director. Maya tells about her own experiences as an African American woman in her writings. She has written many books. Here are some quotes from Maya Angelou. They talk about life, friendship, and family.

"Life truly does give back, many times over, what you put into it."

"Your life is much more important than you could imagine. It is your first treasure."

"Live life as if it were created just for you."

"A friend stands beside you and under you and lifts you up."

"You cannot use up creativity. The more you use, the more you have."

"We are living art, created to hang on, stand up, forbear, continue, and encourage others."

"It is not that I have confidence, but I believe if I fail, so what? Now I have the chance to try again."

"No one comes from the earth like grass. We come like trees. We all have roots."

"Families remind me of giant redwoods, shading the small trees that grow at their feet."

Maya Angelou

How did I read?	How can I do better?

Vowel Sounds

1. Write each word from the box to complete the chart.
    Some words may fit in more than one category.

life	give	back	many	create	over
under	use	trees	glow	more	all

Long vowels	Short vowels	Long o
_____	_____	_____
_____	_____	_____
_____	_____	
_____	_____	
_____	_____	
_____	_____	

Draw a Picture

2. Choose one quote and draw your own picture about it.

Knock, Knock Jokes

Knock, Knock
    Who's there?
Danielle!
        Danielle who?
Danielle so loud, I heard you the first time!

Knock, Knock
    Who's there?
Idaho!
        Idaho who?
Idaho'd the whole garden but I was tired!

Knock, Knock
    Who's there?
Radio!
        Radio who?
Radio not, here I come!

Authors unknown

How did I read?	How can I do better?
☺ ☺ ☹	

Vowel sounds

1. Which words from the selection have **Long o** vowel sounds?
Use each one in a sentence.

_____

_____

_____

_____

_____

_____

What Does It Mean?

2. The answers to Knock, Knock jokes sound like other words.
Write what each phrase stands for.

Danielle

_____

Idaho'd

_____

Radio

_____

Monster Jokes

What did the monster say when he saw a rush-hour
train full of passengers?

    Oh good! A chew chew train!

How do you greet a three-headed monster?

    Hello, hello, hello!

What kind of monster has the best hearing?

    The eeriest!

Why are monsters forgetful?

    Because everything goes in one ear and out the others!

What has a purple-spotted body, four elephant legs,
and big eyes on stalks?

    I don't know either but there is
    one right behind you!

Authors unknown

How did I read?	How can I do better?

Search for Words

1. Write a word from the Monster Jokes that is a synonym
for each of these.

chomp, bite _____   large _____

scariest _____   traveler _____

welcome _____

2. Some compound words are made of two different words joined
by a dash. For example, "The pitcher is **left-handed**." List three
compound words like this from the Monster Jokes.

_____   _____   _____

Draw a Monster

3. Draw a picture of a monster in the box. Then write a
sentence that uses adjectives to describe your monster.

Bought Me a Cat

Bought me a cat and the cat pleased me,
I fed my cat under yonder tree.
Cat goes fiddle-i-fee.

Bought me a hen and the hen pleased me,
I fed my hen under yonder tree.
Hen goes chimmy-chuck, chimmy-chuck,
Cat goes fiddle-i-fee.

Bought me a duck and the duck pleased me,
I fed my duck under yonder tree.
Duck goes quack, quack,
Hen goes chimmy-chuck, chimmy-chuck,
Cat goes fiddle-i-fee.

Bought me a goose and the goose pleased me
I fed my goose under yonder tree.
Goose goes hissy, hissy,
Duck goes quack, quack,
Hen goes chimmy-chuck, chimmy-chuck,
Cat goes fiddle-i-fee.

Bought me a cow and the cow pleased me,
I fed my cow under yonder tree.
Cow goes moo, moo,
Goose goes hissy, hissy,
Duck goes quack, quack,
Hen goes chimmy-chuck, chimmy-chuck,
Cat goes fiddle-i-fee.

Traditional rhyme

How did I read?	How can I do better?
☺ ☺ ☹	

Who Says What?

1. Write what the animals in the song say.

cow   _____

goose   _____

duck   _____

hen   _____

cat   _____

Alike

2. Write a sentence that tells one way that a cat and a cow are alike.

_____

_____

3. Write a sentence that tells one way the hen, duck, and goose are alike.

_____

_____

Old Joe Clark

Old Joe Clark, he had a house
Eighteen stories high
Ev'ry story in that house
Was filled with chicken pie

Fare ye well, Old Joe Clark
Fare ye well, I say
Fare ye well, Old Joe Clark
I'm a-goin' away

I went down to Old Joe's house
Stayed to have some supper
Stubbed my toe on the table leg
And stuck my nose in the butter

Fare ye well, Old Joe Clark
Fare ye well, I say
Fare ye well, Old Joe Clark
I'm a-goin' away

Raccoon has a bushy tail
'Possum's tail is bare
Rabbit has no tail at all
'Cept a bunch of hair

Fare ye well, Old Joe Clark
Fare ye well, I say
Fare ye well, Old Joe Clark
I'm a-goin' away

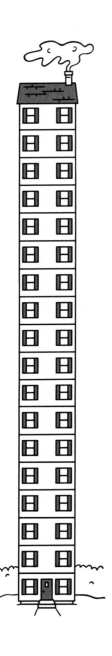

Traditional song

How did I read?	How can I do better?

Rhyming Words

1. The song has three pairs of rhyming words. Write each pair.

_____   _____

_____   _____

_____   _____

Answer This

2. How tall is Old Joe's house? _____

3. Why did the speaker go to Old Joe's house? _____

4. What happens to the speaker at Old Joe's house? _____

_____

Draw a Picture

5. Draw a picture showing the different tails for Raccoon, 'Possum, and Rabbit.

from The Velveteen Rabbit

There was once a velveteen rabbit, and in the beginning he was really splendid. He was fat and bunchy, as a rabbit should be; his coat was spotted brown and white, he had real thread whiskers, and his ears were lined with pink sateen.

For a long time he lived in the toy cupboard or on the nursery floor, and no one thought very much about him. He was naturally shy, and being only made of velveteen, some of the more expensive toys quite snubbed him. The mechanical toys were very superior, and looked down upon everyone else; they were full of modern ideas, and pretended they were real. The model boat, who had lived through two seasons and lost most of his paint, caught the tone from them and never missed an opportunity of referring to his rigging in technical terms. The Rabbit could not claim to be a model of anything, for he didn't know that real rabbits existed; he thought they were all stuffed with sawdust like himself, and he understood that sawdust was quite out-of-date and should never be mentioned in modern circles. Even Timothy, the jointed wooden lion, who was made by the disabled soldiers, and should have had broader views, put on airs.

Between them all the poor little Rabbit was made to feel himself very insignificant and commonplace, and the only person who was kind to him at all was the Skin Horse.

Margery Williams

Word Meanings

1. Write each word or phrase from the poem after
   its definition.

> | put on airs | opportunity | snubbed | rigging |
> | out-of-date | nursery | commonplace |

chance _____

ignored _____

room where babies or toddlers live _____

act as if one is better than others _____

old fashioned _____

ropes used to raise sails _____

ordinary _____

Story Questions

2. What does the Velveteen Rabbit look like?

_____

3. What problem does he have?

_____

from The Wind in the Willows

Chapter I: The River Bank

The Mole had been working very hard all the morning, spring-cleaning his little home. First with brooms, then with dusters; then on ladders and steps and chairs, with a brush and a pail of whitewash; till he had dust in his throat and eyes, and splashes of whitewash all over his black fur, and an aching back and weary arms. Spring was moving in the air above and in the earth below and around him, penetrating even his dark and lowly little house with its spirit of divine discontent and longing. It was small wonder, then, that he suddenly flung down his brush on the floor, said, "Bother!... Hang spring-cleaning!" and bolted out of the house without even waiting to put on his coat. Something up above was calling him imperiously, and he made for the steep little tunnel which answered in his case to the gravelled carriage-drive owned by animals whose residences are nearer to the sun and air. So he scraped and scratched and scrabbled and scrooged and then he scrooged again and scrabbled and scratched and scraped, working busily with his little paws and muttering to himself, "Up we go! Up we go!" till at last, pop! his snout came out into the sunlight, and he found himself rolling in the warm grass of a great meadow.

Kenneth Grahame

How did I read?	How can I do better?

Write Antonyms

1. Write an antonym from the box for each of these
   words from *The Wind in the Willows.*

yelling	below	lazily	easy	dawdled	light	huge	still

small _____   above _____

muttering _____   bolted _____

moving _____   busily _____

hard _____   dark _____

Story Questions

2. Who is the character in the story?

_____

3. What is he doing at first?

_____

4. What does he do at the end?

_____

5. Why does he do those things?

_____

from The Jungle Book

The bushes rustled a little in the thicket, and Father Wolf dropped with his haunches under him, ready for his leap. Then, if you had been watching, you would have seen the most wonderful thing in the world—the wolf checked in mid-spring. He made his bound before he saw what it was he was jumping at, and then he tried to stop himself. The result was that he shot up straight into the air for four or five feet, landing almost where he left ground.

"Man!" he snapped. "A man's cub. Look!"

Directly in front of him, holding on by a low branch, stood a baby who could just walk—as soft and as dimpled a little atom as ever came to a wolf's cave at night. He looked up into Father Wolf's face, and laughed.

"Is that a man's cub?" said Mother Wolf. "I have never seen one. Bring it here."

Father Wolf's jaws closed right on the child's back. Not a tooth even scratched the skin as he laid it down among the cubs.

"How little! How bold!" said Mother Wolf softly. The baby was pushing his way between the cubs to get close to the warm hide. "Ahai! He is taking his meal with the others. And so this is a man's cub. Now, was there ever a wolf that could boast of a man's cub among her children?"

Rudyard Kipling

How did I read?	How can I do better?
☺ ☺ ☹	

More Than One

1. Words that end in **-ch** or **-sh** form their plurals by adding **-es**. Find words in the selection that make plural forms by adding **-es**. Write them below.

   _____   _____   _____

2. Now write more words you know that end in **-ch** or **-sh** and form plurals by adding **-es**. Write the word and the plural form on the lines.

   _____   _____

   _____   _____

Hey, Baby!

3. What word in the story means "baby wolf"?

   _____

4. Draw a line from the animal name to the name of the animal's baby.

sheep	colt
cow	calf
horse	puppy
bear	piglet
dog	lamb
pig	cub

A Counting-Out Song

What is the song the children sing,
When doorway lilacs bloom in Spring,
And the schools are loosed, and the games are played
That were deadly earnest when Earth was made?
Hear them chattering, shrill and hard,
After dinner-time, out in the yard,
As the sides are chosen and all submit
To the chance of the lot that shall make them "It."
"Eeney, Meeney, Miney, Mo!
Catch a tiger by the toe!
(If he hollers let him go!)
Eeney, Meeney, Miney, Mo!
You-are-It!"

Rudyard Kipling

How did I read?	How can I do better?
☺ ☺ ☹	

Two Ts, Please

1. Find a word in the poem that has a **double t**.
Write it on the line.

_____

2. Write four more words you know that also have a **double t**.

_____   _____

_____   _____

Look What I've Caught!

3. Look at this line from the poem:

Catch a tiger by the toe!

Notice that **tiger** and **toe** begin with the same letter. Replace
these two words with other words that also begin with the
same letter. The first word should be an animal. The second
word should be a part of the animal's body. The first one is
done for you.

Catch a _____**billy goat**_____ by the _____**beard**_____!

Catch a _____ by the _____!

Catch a _____ by the _____!

Catch a _____ by the _____!

Catch a _____ by the _____!

from The Song of the Jellicles

Jellicle Cats come out tonight
Jellicle Cats come one, come all;
The Jellicle Moon is shining bright—
Jellicles come to the Jellicle Ball.

Jellicle Cats are black and white,
Jellicle Cats are rather small;
Jellicle Cats are merry and bright,
And pleasant to hear when they caterwaul.
Jellicle Cats have cheerful faces,
Jellicle Cats have bright black eyes;
They like to practice their airs and their graces
And wait for the Jellicle Moon to rise.

T. S. Eliot

How did I read?	How can I do better?
☺ ☺ ☹	

Make a Word Ladder

1. Change the word **black** into a new word.

Remove one letter from black to make the opposite of front._____

Change the last sound in the new
word. Name something you use to hit a ball. _____

Change the first consonant in the
new word. Name what this selection is about. _____

Write Opposites

2. Write a word from the poem that is the opposite of each word below.

dark _____

big _____

awful _____

sad _____

Draw a Picture

3. Read the poem again. Then draw a Jellicle cat.

Wise Words from William Shakespeare

Neither a borrower, nor a lender be;
For loan oft loses both itself and friend.

Hamlet

This above all: to thine own self be true,
And it must follow, as the night the day,
Thou canst not then be false to any man.

Hamlet

All the world's a stage
and all the men and women merely players;
They have their exits and entrances;
And one man in his time plays many parts.

As You Like It

How did I read?	How can I do better?
☺ ☺ ☹	

Nouns and Verbs

1. Look at this phrase from the first quotation.
   Then answer the questions.

   Neither a borrower, nor a lender be;

   A borrower is someone who _____.

   A lender is someone who _____.

2. Now write more sentences in the same form. Use words
   that include **-er** at the end of an action verb.

   A _____er is someone who _____.

   A _____er is someone who _____.

   A _____er is someone who _____.

   A _____er is someone who _____.

   A _____er is someone who _____.

   A _____er is someone who _____.

What Does It Mean?

3. Choose one saying from William Shakespeare and write
   it in your own words.

   _____

   _____

   _____